EVOLUTION OF BUSINESS ENTERPRISES IN TAMIL NADU

AN OVERVIEW

PAUL ARUN

ISBN 978-1-63940-749-1

Contents

Preface

Entrepreneurship was, I would say, unjustly viewed as a contagious and dangerous disease in post-independence India with strong belief and roots in socialism.

But in the decades that followed the Indian Government's attitude of *'throwing the baby out with the bathwater'* dissipated along with the illogical myth that economic goals could be more effectively achieved and escalated productively by Government rather than business.

In short, the *"the trust-deficit"* slowly but surely evaporated and eventually went *'off the radar'*.

In spite of the humungous challenges, Indian business communities even when trampled and undervalued shrugged of the *'proverbial snub'* and played an unforgettable and pivotal role in preserving and nurturing the country's lofty entrepreneurial tradition.

The objective of this narrative is to showcase the evolution of business enterprise in Tamil Nadu amidst the travails and inherent lacunae into a mature, pro-active segment toseamlessly transition and adopt, augment infrastructure, investment, job creation and playing a productive and pivotal role in the overall development of our beloved nation.

I will be touching upon the players *(community-wise demarcation for better understanding)* who were big-time involved in the creation of a vibrant and resourceful business-landscape heralding hope, growth and revenues as also contributing to the GDP of our nation in a stellar way.

Rewinding to the 50's and propelling the narrative to the current context, this is an attempt to look through the background of various 'movers and shakers' in TN thereby instilling a nostalgic reminiscence of how far the decades-old edifice has facilitated a seamless and smooth transition spanning multiple decades from the 'languishing' to the 'flourishing' mode of today's business *'achievers and performers'* who would be the first to gratefully concede deserving credit to the yesteryear legends for the exponential growth being witnessed today.

ACKNOWLEDGEMENTS

All the peers and various stakeholders from whom I learnt the trade and not the *'trick of the trade'*

I

Tamil Brahmins (Tambrams)

Predominantly recognized and acknowledged for academic pursuits and focusing on service government postings, the other side of their entrepreneurial personality was that of uncanny business acumen noteworthy and producing stellar-supremos' in the TN business landscape.

True they had a distinct advantage in English education, the master key for opening the doors to the profession and service appointments.

From a business viewpoint, initially they ventured into money lending business, the torchbearer being the family of Iyers from the village Kallidakurichi near Tirunelveli and branching out to banking and financial service sector – a logical and well-thought out move to diversify.

The Tambram entry into industry in the 1920's was spearheaded by Seshayee Brothers *(R.Seshayee & V.Seshayee – not related incidentally)* starting with transportation services and upkeep & service of buses, cars and motorcycles.

As years progressed the Seshayee group evolved into a **magnus**-opus conglomerate venturing into production of caustic soda, bleaching powder and chlorine through **Mettur Chemicals and Industrial Corporation in Salem.**

Enter Caption

The other notable luminary and trailblazer was indisputably

Enter Caption

T.V.Sundaram Iyengar with interests in sales & service of automobiles and setting up of macro-giant institutions like Wheels India, Lucas TVS, Brakes India *(no need for introduction)* to name few from their ever-blooming stable of institutions. Their relevance in today's business context is profound and a successful figurehead in the overall template of business mechanism and dynamics.

Followed closely by S.Anandaramakrishnan who, to begin with, joined the board of Simpson & Co as Company secretary. It was at this point in time Simpson well-entrenched in coach-and-carriage building domain was expanding its business horizon by diversifying into harnesses, saddler and billiards table verticals and also distribution and servicing of imported automobiles – a *'niche'* segment those days.

Higginbothams, Stanes & Co and a few more prudent buy-outs established their firm foothold in TN business roadmap auguring and heralding a multi-dimensional growth of their group of Institutions.

Exponential growth in the form of M & A*(mergers and acquisitions)*, ensured aggressive expansion and the end-result was bringing India Pistons, TAFE and Eicher Motors among other blue-chip companies into their already-burgeoning entrepreneurial excellence.

Enter Caption

No need for introduction of the *'fourth estate'* powerhouse in the South 'The Hindu' – an Iyengar concern founded by G.Subramania Aiyer percolating right down to S.Kasthuri Ranga Iyengar a lawyer form Kumbakonam. Till now as all of us know, N.Ram and the entire team of 'The Hindu' is viewed with reverence for maintaining and upholding high standards of journalistic ethics and values coupled with accuracy and neutrality indispensable traits in the publishing sector. Classic case study for longevity in business affairs.

Last but not the least, TTK Group lead by Krishnamachari starting with Unilever distributorship and foraying into politics culminating in him being made Union Finance Minister in the late 1950's.

Also the TTK Group focused on FMCG manufacture and their *'top of the world'* portfolio included but not limited to *'Prestige'* pressure cookers, *'Woodwards gripe water'*, *'Tantex'*, *'Kiwi'* shoe polish, *'Brylcream'* and

'Kohinoor' condoms.

The intriguing fact was they were unable to leverage their admirable brand-equity to escalate growth to the pinnacle though it was planned and perceived to achieve the apex goal.

From a social responsibility perspective, TTK's daughter-in-law

Enter Caption

Mrs.Shanthi Ranganathan started the TTK Hospital for de-addiction and rehabilitation in 1980 and serving countless number of suffering alcoholic and addict patients and families establishing themselves as the benchmark and figurehead in the rehab vertical.

II

Kongunad Naidus and Gounders

Coimbatore justifiably accredited with the moniker *'Manchester of South India'* is referred to as the *'Light Engineering powerhouse of India'*.

Colloquially it is rightly said, any person willing to be honest and puts in conscientious efforts can survive and become successful in Coimbatore. Such is the immense potential to grow that is offered by this hospitable and pleasant city surrounded by hills stations and exotic locales to whet the eager-beaver appetite of the *'in demand'* tourist populace.

Legendary, potent and influential leaders from the Naidu and Gounder community are jointly responsible for the elite status Coimbatore enjoys within the TN business landscape and pan-India as well.

Astonishing fact is CBE though no endowed and blessed with environmental and infrastructure richness and support like Bombay or Calcutta. Add-on CBE has not reaped the concomitant economic benefits enjoyed by its *'big cousins'* showered with limitless largesse of being a political or admin HQ or the status of a financial capital.

Despite these obviously deterrent infirmities, CBE has emerged as a land of foundries, machine shops, engineering units and, most importantly, evolved into a major engineering and automotive hub like the TVS group and Amalgamations in Chennai. *(as we saw in the outset)*

In short, the gradual progression of business dominance is because of the holistic efforts of the Kongunad Naidu's and Gounder's. More so though the primary vocation was farming they were deprived of an agro-climatic region buttressed by perennial rivers and munificent monsoons.

Movers & Shakers

'Accomplishers par-excellence'

G.K.Naidu, his son G.K.Sundaram- dynamic entrepreneurswith inherent business acumen, skills, far-sighted vision and a pro-active approach founded

Enter Caption

Lakshmi Mills a gargantuan business **behemoth/conglomerate** with long-lasting impact on the city's economic map and contextually very-relevant as also

Enter Caption

P.S.G.Naiduwho floated the first-ever Naidu-owned textile mill.

Both groups endeavored and labored earnestly to create a platform for mushrooming business enterprises and predominantly credited to CBE earning the much-envied status of emerging as a mini-Manchester.

In the stupendous sojourn they embarked a century ago they have associated themselves with establishing 'big-ticket' educational institutions to serve the aspiring and budding academic talent of the whole country.

Engineering excellence

One enduring symbol of CBE's engineering ethos is

G.D.Naidu who developed the country's first indigenous electric motor way back in 1939 even before the Kirloskar Brothers. Shining torchbearer of the community aptly named as 'Thomas Alva Edison of India', left an indelible imprint in various verticals mainly manufacture of many consumer durable goods under the titular umbrella of UMS (United Motor service) Group.

Following in the illustrious footsteps of G.D.Naidu were D.Balasundaram (Textool), Narayanaswamy Naidu and equally-significant others acting as a trendsetting catalyst to foster a culture of industrial research and shop floor innovation which became a distinguishable hallmark of CBE.

Balasundaram's inventive zeal was emulated by his son B.Jayachandran whose Jaya Automobiles has the distinction of developing the first indigenous diesel engines for the *'Ambassador' 'Premier Padmini'* and *'Standard 2000'* cars besides rolling out India's first own car named *'Mayura'* in 1986.

Much of the region's strength is derived from its foundries and skilled human resource base thereby creating a manufacturing haven for auto components, light engineering goods among other domain.

The Naidu-effect will not be complete without mentioning the incomparable contribution of the

Enter Caption

KG Group *(K.Govindaswamy Naidu)*. Multifariousinterests in entertainment, healthand education sectors to name a fewhas evolved into a fully-integrated textile major with *'top of the tier'*brands like Sharadha Terry products, K.G.Denim Ltd and Trigger jeans.

Othe high-impact contributors' from the Naidu community are R.Ramaswamy *(paper plants)*, B.Soundararajan *(Suguna poultry)*, V.Lakshmi Narayanaswamy *(Suguna Industries)*, R.R.Ranganathan *(Ellen Industries)* and many more stalwarts.

Gounder *(Exquisite and magnificient)*

Comparatively late entrants into industry sphere – 1930's. Origin being progressive agriculturists and the fountainhead was Vellingar Gounder *(Kaleeswari Mills)*, Kandasamy and Rathnasabapathy Gounder.

Almost 3 decades later, Karunambikar Mills *(Ramana Gounder)* and

Enter Caption

Sri Sakthi Textiles*(Pollachi **N.Mahalingam)***made a profound impact in the overall entrepreneur canvas of CBE and diversified further into other regions of TN.

Conglomerate of Sakthi Group boasts of unparalleled interests in sugar, transport, finance, auto components, textiles, education and edible oil verticals. Their pulsating performance across domains has ensured they are a household name in TN if not pan- India.

Analyze the dominance of the Gounders from the beginning, the circle won't be complete without broaching the awe-inspiring presence of Tirupur city which displaced traditional knitwear export clusters such as Bombay, Ludhiana and Delhi to propel to the *'numero uno'* position across India giving a run for the money to established giants nationwide.

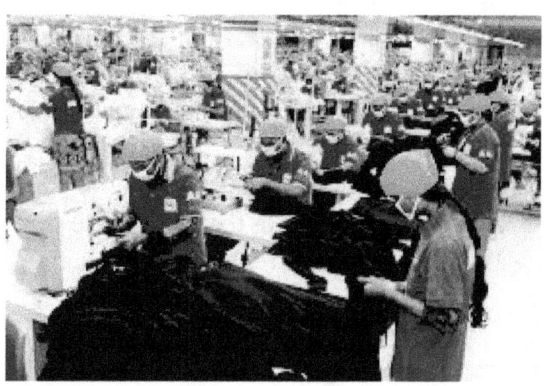

Enter Caption

Tirupur *(India's banian capital)*rose up like a phoenix to unprecedented heights of achievement culminating in its product portfolio expansion from 'basic' T-Shirts to more fashion-intensive sportswear, Bermudas, lingerie etc predominantly catering to big-ticket global buyers like C&A, Wal-Mart, Tommy Hilfiger, GAP and many such internationally-acclaimed brands.

Other notable contributors being Srishanmughavel group *(textile baron – P.S.Velusamy)*, KPR Group *(K.P.Ramasamy)*, Royal Classic Group *(Classic Polo & Smash brands)* – the list is endless and their exponential growth necessitated their penetration into other regions like Dindigul, Erode and satellite towns such as Tirupur and Annur.

Add-on

Palani G.Periasamy

business honchos like Palani G.Periasamy *(Dharani Sugars and Le'Royal Meridien, Chennai, PGP College of education & technology, Namakkal)* and a entrepreneur of recent vintage – M.Ramasami *(seed business – tie-up with Mahyco and Mahindra seeds)*.

To sum-up Naidu and Gounder businessmen have supplemented each other's progress and prosperity despite the irrevocable fact that the Naidu textile bastion was, in an act of entrepreneurial subterfuge, subjected to aggressive Gounder encroachment from the fringes fortunately with no heavy casualties.

Otherwise the probability of a *'commercial cold-war'* between the bigwigs would have resulted in a catastrophe decimating CBE's aspiration of becoming a vibrant and forceful business region impacting the nation and international business-map.

III

Nadars

Powerful presence in Southern TN specifically Tirunelveli, Tiruchendur Kanyakumari and Thoothukudi where it was a monopoly literally.

Early birds were

A.V.Thomas *(AVT group- 1925)* and **V. G. Panneerdas***(1955)*

A. V. Thomas *(AVT group- 1925)* and **V. G. Panneerdas***(1955)*

Building an edifice in the above-mentioned towns they geographically expanded to neighbouring areas like Sivakasi, Virudhunagar, Sattankudi and many more high-potential towns.

Nadars are a business community in the true sense of the word. To explain, even today they are looked up in awe for their *'no-nonsense'* approach to business and fair practices which is second to none.

Financial muscle coupled with self-confidence and assertive attitude *(genetic blessing, perhaps!)* brought to the table in their business activities from their social and economic backdrop and resulted in excellent track record which percolated down their generations for years to come.

Another town that flourished was

Enter Caption

Sivakasi which was proving to be productive hub and as a logical extension business boomed. Proof of the vast potential waiting to be exploited there, many start-ups came into being, noteworthy among them being National Litho Printing Press, Sivakasi Industrial Printing Works, Coronation Litho Works Ltd and Eagle Press well-known entity in Madras.

But the crème de la crème is the Srinivas Fine Arts Group which launched the world's most expensive diary'SilverOak Diary' astronomically priced at a whopping amount of Rs.57, 000/-(R.Chockalingam) and sold a record 300 copies in 2004.

Moving on to Virudhunagar, a strong Nadar-belt for decades, production of sesame oil was taken up by 4 brothers in the late 1930's – Shanmuga

Nadar, Vanniaperumal, Dhanushkodi Nadar and V.V.Ramasami who further branched out to establish separate businesses.

Dhanushkodi Nadar's VVD group based at Thoothukudi, Munusamy*(Kaleeswari Refinery Pvt Ltd)* manufactures of popular Gold Winner, R.G.Chandramogan *(Hatsun Foods)*,

Satchet Supremo!

C.K.Ranganathan *(Cavin Kare)*who changed the dynamics in the personal hygiene products vertical by introducing 'satchet' concept and many more*'movers and shakers'*.

Not to be left out are trendsetters like

Enter Caption

Vasanth Kumar, Rajagopal Nadar and the incomparable

Enter Caption

B.Sivanthi Adityan *(Daily Thanthi group)*and global-achiever Shiv Nadar *(HCL)*.

As a final rundown on this dynamic and self-motivated community, special mention must be made of

Enter Caption

V. G. Panneerdas the founder of <u>VGP Group of Companies</u>, a poor man from a remote village called Azhagappa puram in the Tirunelveli District. He moved to <u>Chennai</u>in search of opportunities and in 1955 opened a shop selling items such as alarm clocks, watches and wall clocks.Pioneer in South India to introduce Hire Purchase for everyday goods, he single-handedly built the VGP company from virtually nothing to its present status as a group of companies including retail, real estate and property development, resorts and amusement parks *(including <u>VGP Universal Kingdom</u>)* and video and audio studios.

To summarize, the ever-ebullient Nadar community was/is a potent contributor to TN's economy with political backdrop and are omnipresent in every tier of enterprise and business activity.

IV

Chettiars

Highlight of TN's business fraternity would be incongruous without showcasing the invaluable contribution of the Chettiar community to overall business development.

Business skills in the bloodline supplemented by the enviable zeal, passion and the uncanny ability to forecast and identify *'million-dollar'* opportunities and instinctively pounce on it were some of the admirable traits inherent and percolating right down generations.

Needless to mention, there were *'shining stars'* with rags to riches storyline imitated and transcending parameters of region and community. In short, in my humble opinion, it would not be untrue to ever they are the southern version of the Marwari and Jain community.

Financial service powerhouses:

Fountainhead of the community, Sir R.A.Chettiar promoted the Indian Bank and Bank of Chettinad – Rangoon and

Enter Caption

followed closely by M.C.T.M.Chettiar's family-controlled I.O.B and United Life Assurance Company and A.M.Murugappa Chettiar with blue-chip Institutions like Tube Products, TI Cycles, Cholamandalam General Insurance and other *'winners'*.

Niche and power-packed business barons which also includes Thiagaraja Chettiar *(Loyal Textiles, Bank of Madura etc)* to complete the circle of awe-inspiring *'fore steppers and accomplishers'*.

V

Marquee Maestro's of TN Business

To bring the curtain down on this narrative, it would be unfair to forget the lasting legacy created and sustained by the yesteryear luminaries which is being carried forward by the current-gen entrepreneurs who have taken the world by storm.

Yes today's *hi-wheeling'* and *globetrotting* businesspersons have embraced the basic tenet fashioned and considered as sacrosanct by the *'golden oldies'* and incorporated their distinct imprint to fly high and are pivotal to the progressive economic growth of Mother India. Yesterday's legacy is the springboard upon which they giant-leap forward with the singular passion and focus of being a major influencer as part of the pan-India group and ensure we are on *'top of the world'* in world commerce and economics by Year 2030.

Business magnates like Senapathy Kris Gopalakrishnan *(recipient of the Padma Bhushan award),*

Enter Caption

Venu Srinivasan(TN's pride - Deming Distinguished Service Award, Life Time Achievement Award, Champion of Champions and Best CEO, Goodwill Envoy for Public Diplomacy, Doctor of Management, Ishikawa-Kano Award, J R D Tata Corporate Leadership Award, and Jamsetji Tata Lifetime Achievement Award,

Enter Caption

Kalanithi Maran (all-powerful Sun Group) to name a few.

VI

In Conclusion

Apart from the 5 bigwig community-contributors to overall *(economic,education & social)* development of TN, there have been zillion traders and entrepreneurs who have been the backbone and edifice upon which the humungous building was founded and growing by leaps and bounds.

In the next volume, I would be, in details, sharing about the entrepreneurs who have made a difference since Y2K.

www.ingramcontent.com/pod-product-compliance
Lightning Source LLC
Chambersburg PA
CBHW061522180526
45171CB00001B/291